WORDS

by

Robert Creeley

WORDS

Poems by Robert Creeley

CHARLES SCRIBNER'S SONS · NEW YORK

for Bobbie
— anymore

Grateful acknowledgement is made to the following publications in which some of these poems first appeared:

Agenda; Arbor; Beloit Poetry Journal; Broadside Poems #6; Burning Deck; Coyote's Journal; Choice; El Corno Emplumado; Encounter; Evergreen Review; Fubbalo; Fuck You: A Magazine of the Arts; The Genre of Silence; Granta; Grist; King Ida's Watch Chain; Lugano Review; My Own Mag; The Nation; Niagara Frontier Review; A Nosegay in Black; Origin; Oyez; Paris Review; Poetry; The Resuscitator; Wild Dog; Writing; and the Yale Literary Magazine.

Acknowledgement is also made to Gemini G.E.L. for the poems used in its publication *About Women* (in collaboration with John Altoon), to the Goliard Press (London) for its publication of "A Sight" (in collaboration with R. B. Kitaj), and to The Perishable Press Ltd. for the poems used in *Words* (a much abbreviated earlier edition of this present book, printed privately).

Finally, I should like to thank The John Simon Guggenheim Memorial Foundation for a fellowship, and The Rockefeller Foundation for a grant in writing—both of which were of significant help to me.

Things continue, but my sense is that I have, at best, simply taken place with that fact. I see no progress in time or any other such situation. So it is that what I feel, in the world, is the one thing I know myself to be, for that instant. I will never know myself otherwise.

Intentions are the variability of all these feelings, moments of that possibility. How can I ever assume that they must come to this or that substance? I am trying to say that what I think to say is of no help to me—and yet insist on my seriousness, which is a sense of my nature I would like to admire.

Words will not say anything more than they do, and my various purposes will not understand them more than what they say.

R. C.

Contents

I

II

There is, in short,
a counter stress,
    born of the sexual shock,
        which survives it
consonant with the moon,
    to keep its own mind.

W. C. WILLIAMS

I

THE RHYTHM

It is all a rhythm,
from the shutting
door, to the window
opening,

the seasons, the sun's
light, the moon,
the oceans, the
growing of things,

the mind in men
personal, recurring
in them again,
thinking the end

is not the end, the
time returning,
themselves dead but
someone else coming.

If in death I am dead,
then in life also
dying, dying . . .
And the women cry and die.

The little children
grow only to old men.
The grass dries,
the force goes.

But is met by another
returning, oh not mine,
not mine, and
in turn dies.

The rhythm which projects
from itself continuity
bending all to its force
from window to door,
from ceiling to floor,
light at the opening,
dark at the closing.

THE ROCKS

Trying to think of
some way out, the
rocks of thought

which displace,
dropped in
the water,

much else.
So life is
water, love also

has substance of
like kind.
Wanting

water a Sunday
morning God will
not provide—

is it my
wife, her warmth
lying

beside me, is
that sense of warm
moistness the condition

in which all grows?
Drop
the rock,

think well, think
well of me.

WATER

The sun's
sky in
form of
blue sky
that

water will
never make
even
in
reflection.

Sing, song,
mind's form
feeling
if
mistaken,

shaken,
broken water's
forms, love's
error
in water.

THE MOUNTAINS
IN THE DESERT

The mountains blue now
at the back of my head,
such geography of self and soul
brought to such limit of sight,

I cannot relieve it
nor leave it, my mind locked
in seeing it
as the light fades.

Tonight let me go
at last out of whatever
mind I thought to have,
and all the habits of it.

WAITING

He pushes behind the words
which, awkward, catch
and turn him to a disturbed
and fumbling man.

What if it all stops.
Then silence
is as silence was
again.

What if the last time
he was moved to touch,
work out in his own mind,
such limits was the last—

and then a quiet, a dull
space of hanging actions, all
depending on some time
has come and gone.

God help him then
if such things can.
That risk
is all there is.

THE INVITATION

If it ever is
as it will be,
then enough is
enough. They

think in clusters
round the interminable
subject all but
lost to my mind.

Well, here I am,
they say, together.
Or here you are,
them, and it.

Let's build a house of
human pieces, arms
and hair, not telling
any one. Shout

from the feet, face
facts as accumulations,
we can
do it.

Or and, and as
it's done, what flesh
can do, home again
we'll say,

we'll fall down streets
rolling,
balls
of clear substance.

THE TURN

Each way the turn
twists, to be apprehended:
now she is
there, now she

is not, goes, but
did she, having gone,
went before
the eye saw

nothing. The tree
cannot walk, all its
going must
be violence. They listen

to the saw cut, the
roots scream. And in eating
even a stalk of celery
there will be pathetic screaming.

But what we want
is not what we get.
What we saw, we think
we will see again?

We will not. Moving,
we will
move, and then
stop.

FOR W. C. W.

The rhyme is after
all the repeated
insistence.

There, you say, and
there, and there,
and *and* becomes

just so. And
what one wants is
what one wants,

yet complexly
as you
say.

Let's
let it go.
I want—

Then there is—
and,
I want.

SONG

The grit
of things,
a measure
resistant—

times walk-
ing, talk-
ing, telling
lies and

all the other
places, no
one ever
quite the same.

THE FIRE

Oh flame falling, as shaken, as the stories
my daughter sees in the light, forming, seeing
the simple burning as an action which to speak of
now I complicate, with my own burning, her story.

Then it all goes, saying, here they were, and are,
and will be again, as I used to think, to remember,
then they were here, and now, again, they are.

What in the light's form finds her face,
makes of her eyes the simple grace.

FOR NO CLEAR REASON

I dreamt last night
the fright was over, that
the dust came, and then water,
and women and men, together
again, and all was quiet
in the dim moon's light.

A paean of such patience—
laughing, laughing at me,
and the days extend over
the earth's great cover,
grass, trees, and flower-
ing season, for no clear reason.

THE MESSENGERS

for Allen Ginsberg

The huge dog, Broderick, and
the smile of the quick eyes
of Allen light a kind world.

Their feelings, under some distance
of remote skin, must touch,
wondering at what impatience does

block them. So little love
to share among so many, so much
yellow-orange hair, on the one,

and on the other, such a darkness
of long hanging hair now, such
slightness of body, and a voice that

rises on the sounds of feeling.
Aie! It raises the world, lifts,
falls, like a sudden sunlight, like

that edge of the black night sweeps
the low lying fields, of soft grasses,
bodies, fills them with quiet longing.

FOR LESLIE

For you there ought
to be words as something
at least to say

of what couldn't be
then, the whole
sense crowded, almost

a comfortable agony
so full
I felt it.

Two years go,
the same wide sky
sits over us.

There, the grave is
I cannot
even go to

under some trees
in the grass
of someone's cemetery.

What argument can be
used now, the light so
strikes in,

so blonde you are,
so different from our darkness,
your eyes such blue.

I

"is the grandson
of Thomas L. Creeley, who acquired
eight acres of Belmont land around 1880 and

continued

"His house was numbered 375
Common st.

and his farm lands,
through the heart of which the present Creeley
rd. runs, adjoined

the Chenery holdings and extended
toward Waverly from upper
Common st.
                    The author's father, the late
Dr. Oscar Creeley,
was a prominent Watertown physician
for many years
                    and headed
the staff of Symmes Hospital in Arlington."

I, is late

But I saw a picture of him once, T.L.
in a chair in Belmont, or it was his invalid
and patient wife they told me sat there, he
was standing, long and steady faced,
a burden to him she was, and the son. The
other child had died

They waited, so my father
who also died when I is four gave all
to something like
the word "adjoined," "extended"
so I feels

I sees the time as long and wavering
grass in all about the lot in all that
cemetery again the old man owned a part of
so they couldn't dig him up.

SOMETHING

I approach with such
a careful tremor, always
I feel the finally foolish

question of how it is,
then, supposed to be felt,
and by whom. I remember

once in a rented room on
27th street, the woman I loved
then, literally, after we

had made love on the large
bed sitting across from
a basin with two faucets, she

had to pee but was nervous,
embarrassed I suppose I
would watch her who had but

a moment ago been completely
open to me, naked, on
the same bed. Squatting, her

head reflected in the mirror,
the hair dark there, the
full of her face, the shoulders,

sat spread-legged, turned on
one faucet and shyly pissed. What
love might learn from such a sight.

WALKING

In my head I am
walking but I am not
in my head, where

is there to walk,
not thought of, is
the road itself more

than seen. I think
it might be, feel
as my feet do, and

continue, and
at last reach, slowly,
one end of my intention.

THE LANGUAGE

Locate *I*
love you some-
where in

teeth and
eyes, bite
it but

take care not
to hurt, you
want so

much so
little. Words
say everything,

I
love you
again,

then what
is emptiness
for. To

fill, fill.
I heard words
and words full

of holes
aching. Speech
is a mouth.

THE WINDOW

Position is where you
put it, where it is,
did you, for example, that

large tank there, silvered,
with the white church along-
side, lift

all that, to what
purpose? How
heavy the slow

world is with
everything put
in place. Some

man walks by, a
car beside him on
the dropped

road, a leaf of
yellow color is
going to

fall. It
all drops into
place. My

face is heavy
with the sight. I can
feel my eye breaking.

THE CHANCE

For whatever, it could
be done, simply
remove it, cut the

offending member. Once
in a photograph by
Frederick Sommer a leg

lay on what was apparently
black velvet cut
from its attachment

to the rest, the foot
showing the incised
wound whereof

the beauty
of all
reasons.

HELLO

With a quick
jump he caught
the edge of

her eye and
it tore, down,
ripping. She

shuddered,
with the unexpected
assault, but

to his vantage
he held by
what flesh was left.

QUICK-STEP

More gaily, dance
with such ladies make
a circumstance of dancing.

Let them lead
around and around, all
awkwardness apart.

There is
an easy grace gained
from falling forward

in time, in
simple time to
all their graces.

VARIATIONS

There is love only
as love is. These
senses recreate
their definition—a hand

holds within itself
all reason. The eyes
have seen such
beauty they close.

But continue. So the voice
again, *these senses recreate*
their singular condition
felt, and felt again.

I hear. I hear
the mind close, the voice
go on beyond it,
the hands open.

Hard, they hold so
closely themselves, only,
empty grasping of
such sensation.

Hear, there where
the echoes are
louder, clearer,
senses of sound

opening and closing,
no longer love's
only, mind's intention,
eyes' sight, hands holding—

broken to echoes, *these
senses recreate*
their definition. I hear
the mind close.

THERE IS

There is
as we go we
see there
is a hairy
hole there is
a darkness ex-
panded by
there is a
sense of some
imminence imman-
ence there is
a subject placed
by the verb a
conjunction coord-
inate lines
a graph of indeterminate
feelings there is
sorry for itself
lonely generally
unhappy in its
circumstances.

THE MEASURE

I cannot
move backward
or forward.
I am caught

in the time
as measure.
What we think
of we think of—

of no other reason
we think than
just to think—
each for himself.

THE WOMAN

I have never
clearly given to you
the associations
you have for me, you

with such
divided presence my dream
does not show
you. I do not dream.

I have compounded
these sensations, the
accumulation of the things
left me by you.

Always your
tits, not breasts, but
harsh sudden rises
of impatient flesh

on the chest—is it
mine—which flower
against the vagueness
of the air you move in.

You walk
such a shortness
of intent strides, your
height is so low,

in my hand
I feel the weight
of yours there,
one over one

or both, as you
pivot upon me, the
same weight grown
as the hair, the

second of your attributes,
falls to
cover us. We
couple but lie against

no surface, have
lifted as you again
grow small
against myself, into

the air. The
air the third of
the signs you
are known by: a

quiet, a
soughing silence,
the winds lightly
moved. Then

your
mouth, it
opens not
speaking, touches,

wet, on me. Then
I scream, I
sing such as is
given to me, roar-

ing unheard,
like stark sight
sees itself
inverted

into dark
turned. Onanistic,
I feel around
myself what

you have left me
with, wetness, pools
of it, my skin
drips.

THE PATTERN

As soon as
I speak, I
speaks. It

wants to
be free but
impassive lies

in the direction
of its
words. Let

x equal x, x
also
equals x. I

speak to
hear myself
speak? I

had not thought
that some-
thing had such

undone. It
was an idea
of mine.

THE MECHANIC

Were we now to fall
to our stubborn knees
and sink to rest, my-
self sunk in yours, then

what would hold us
together but uninteresting
weight. Do you believe
love, and how much.

WALLS

Walls are
relief in lifting
themselves. Let

you also
lift yourself,
selves, shelves.

"I KEEP TO MYSELF
SUCH MEASURES . . ."

I keep to myself such
measures as I care for,
daily the rocks
accumulate position.

There is nothing
but what thinking makes
it less tangible. The mind,
fast as it goes, loses

pace, puts in place of it
like rocks simple markers,
for a way only to
hopefully come back to

where it cannot. All
forgets. My mind sinks.
I hold in both hands such weight
it is my only description.

THE DREAM

1

Such perfection
of dream would
first hurt, would

tear impression
from impression
making a fabric

of pain. Then
begin again
its own insistence.

In the dream
I see
two faces turned,

one of which
I assume mine, one
of which I assume.

It is
what I now make
up of it, I cannot see

more than hair
at first, a long
flowing hair there

fits it, faces
toward me as I
in it turn. Then

again pain,
for some reason, why
does it hurt. But

my feeling is,
this is what
you enjoy, so

twist to it while
the eye
of the other

face watches
me in pain. I
do not want what

I want. I dream it
in these two
painful things.

2

Why should she not
be attacked
literally. So

I attack my
mother, break
what I can reach,

the hair,
the thing I
came from.

3

If all women are
mothers, what
are men

standing
in dreams, mine
or theirs,

empty of
all but themselves.
They are so

lonely, unknown
there, I run
for whatever

is not
them, turning
into that consequence

makes me
my mother hating
myself.

4

In the day the
instruction is merely,
stand up. An

old joke relating
to the male
genital—up, up.

At night it
is the complex
as all things

are themselves and
their necessity,
even sexual. So

cunts and cocks
as eyes, noses, mouths,
have their objects:

hermaphrodite, one
sexed, bi-
sected in that lust.

5
What was the dream?
I have forgotten it
if I ever knew it

or dreamed
it more
than thinking. It

was to have been,
it was,
such I thought,

thinking. What
to dream, and what,
and what, to dream.

There was hair,
it hurt, I felt
the pain. I felt I did.

I will not
change into any-
thing you don't

like if
you will stay
with me as you said

you would. Don't
go. Away.
If this is where we are.

ONE WAY

Of the two, one
faces one. In
the air there is

no tremor, no
odor. There is
a house around them,

of wood, of walls.
The mark is silence.
Everything hangs.

As he raises
his hand to
not strike her, as

again his hand
is raised, she has
gone, into another

room. In the room
left by her, he
cannot see himself

as in a mirror, as
a feeling of reflection.
He thinks he thinks,

of something else.
All the locked time,
all the letting go

down into it, as a
locked room, come to.
This time not changed,

but the way of feeling
secured by walls and books,
a picture hanging down,

a center shifted, dust
on all he puts his hand on,
disorder, papers and letters

and accumulations of clothing,
and bedclothes, and under his
feet the rug bunches.

SOME AFTERNOON

Why not ride
with pleasure
and take oneself
as measure,

making the world
tacit description
of what's taken
from it

for no good reason,
the fact only.
There is a world
elsewhere, but here

the tangible faces
smile, breaking
into tangible pieces.
I see

myself and family,
and friends, and
animals attached,
the house, the road,

all go forward
in a huge
flash, shaken
with that act.

Goodbye, goodbye.
Nothing left
after the initial
blast but

some echo like this.
Only the faded
pieces of paper
etc.

ANGER

1

The time is.
The air seems a cover,
the room is quiet.

She moves, she
had moved. He
heard her.

The children
sleep, the dog fed,
the house around them

is open, descriptive,
a truck through the walls,
lights bright there,

glaring, the sudden
roar of its motor, all
familiar impact

as it passed
so close. He
hated it.

But what does she answer.
She moves
away from it.

In all they save,
in the way of his saving
the clutter, the accumulation

of the expected disorder—
as if each dirtiness,
each blot, blurred

happily, gave
purpose, happily—
she is not enough there.

He is angry. His
face grows—as if
a moon rose

of black light,
convulsively darkening,
as if life were black.

It is black.
It is an open
hole of horror, of

nothing as if not
enough there is
nothing. A pit—

which he recognizes,
familiar, sees
the use in, a hole

for anger and
fills it
with himself,

yet watches on
the edge of it,
as if she were

not to be pulled in,
a hand could
stop him. Then

as the shouting
grows and grows
louder and louder

with spaces
of the same open
silence, the darkness,

in and out, him-
self between them,
stands empty and

holding out his
hands to both,
now screaming

it cannot be
the same, she
waits in the one

while the other
moans in the hole
in the floor, in the wall.

2
Is there some odor
which is anger,

a face
which is rage.

I think I think
but find myself in it.

The pattern
is only resemblance.

I cannot see myself
but as what I see, an

object but a man,
with lust for forgiveness,

raging, from that vantage,
secure in the purpose,

double, split.
Is it merely intention,

a sign quickly adapted,
shifted to make

a horrible place
for self-satisfaction.

I rage.
I rage, I rage.

3
You did it,
and didn't want to,

and it was simple.
You were not involved,

even if your head was cut off,
or each finger

twisted
from its shape until it broke,

and you screamed too
with the other, in pleasure.

4
Face me,
in the dark,
my face. See me.

It is the cry
I hear all
my life, my own

voice, my
eye locked in
self sight, not

the world what
ever it is
but the close

breathing beside
me I reach out
for, feel as

warmth in
my hands then
returned. The rage

is what I
want, what
I cannot give

to myself, of
myself, in
the world.

5
After, what
is it—as if
the sun had

been wrong to return,
again. It was
another life, a

day, some
time gone, it
was done.

But also
the pleasure, the
opening

relief
even in what
was so hated.

6
All you say you want
to do to yourself you do
to someone else as yourself

and we sit between you
waiting for whatever will
be at last the real end of you.

DISTANCE

1

Hadn't I been
aching, for you,
seeing the

light there, such
shape as
it makes.

The bodies
fall, have
fallen, open.

Isn't it such
a form one
wants, the warmth

as sun
light on you.
But what

were you, where,
one thought, I
was always

thinking. The
mind itself,
impulse, of form

last realized,
nothing
otherwise but

a stumbling
looking after, a
picture

of light through
dust on
an indeterminate distance,

which throws
a radiator into
edges, shining,

the woman's long
length, the move-
ment of the

child, on her,
their legs
from behind.

2
Eyes,
days and
forms' photograph,

glazed
eyes, dear
hands. We

are walking,
I have
a face grown

hairy
and old, it
has greyed

to white
on the sides
of my cheeks. Stepping

out of
the car with these
endless people,

where are
you, am I happy,
is this car

mine. Another
life comes to
its presence,

here, you
sluffing, beside
me, me off, my-

self's warmth
gone inward,
a stepping

car, walking
waters on, such
a place like the

size of great
breasts, warmth and
moisture, come

forward, waking
to that edge
of the silence.

3
The falling back
from as in
love, or

casual friend-
ship, "I am so
happy, to

meet you—" These
meetings, it is
meet

we right (write)
to one another,
the slip-

shod, half-
felt, heart's
uneasinesses in

particular
forms, waking to
a body felt

as a hand pushed
between the long
legs. Is this

only the form,
"Your face
is unknown to me

but the hair, the
springing hair there
despite the rift,

the cleft,
between us, is
known, my own—"

What have *they*
done to me, who
are they coming

to me on such
informed feet, with
such substance of forms,

pushing
the flesh aside,
step in-

to my own,
my longing
for them.

II

SOME PLACE

I resolved it, I
found in my life a
center and secured it.

It is the house,
trees beyond, a term
of view encasing it.

The weather
reaches only as some
wind, a little

deadened sighing. And
if the life weren't?
when was something to

happen, had I secured
that—had I, *had*
I, insistent.

There is nothing I am,
nothing not. A place
between, I am. I am

more than thought, less
than thought. A house
with winds, but a distance

—something loose in the wind,
feeling weather as that life,
walks toward the lights he left.

SONG

I wouldn't
embarrass you
ever.

If there were
not place
or time for it,

I would go,
go elsewhere,
remembering.

I would
sit in a
flower, a face, not

to embarrass
you, would
be unhappy

quietly, would
never
make a noise.

Simpler,
simpler you
deal with me.

SONG

What do you
want, love. To be
loved. What,

what wanted,
love, wanted
so much as love

like nothing
considered, no
feeling but

a simple
recognition
forgotten sits

in its feeling,
two things,
one and one.

FOR HELEN

      . . . If I can
remember anything, it
is the way ahead
you made for me, specifically:

    wet-
ness, now the grass
as early it
has webs, all the lawn
stretched out from
the door, the back
one with a small crabbed
porch. The trees
are, then, so high,
a huge encrusted
sense of grooved trunk,
I can
slide my finger along
each edge.

A NIGHT SKY

All the grass
dies
in front of us.

The fire
again
flares out.

The night
such a large
place. Stars

the points
but like
places no

depth, I see
a flat—
a plain as if the

desert
were showing smaller
places.

THE ANSWER

Will we speak to each other
making the grass bend as if
a wind were before us, will our

way be as graceful, as
substantial as the movement
of something moving so gently.

We break things in pieces like
walls we break ourselves into
hearing them fall just to hear it.

DIMENSIONS

1

Little places as
size of
one hand, shrink

to one finger
as tall
as, I am

sitting
down even
smaller.

2

Think if
understanding is
what you
had thought

of it, in
it you think
a picture
comes and

goes, re-
flected there
large faces
float but

no harm comes
to the sleeping
princess
ever.

3
My voice is
a foot. My
head is

a foot. I
club
people in

my mind, I
push them this
way, that

way, from
the little
way

I see them
up
the length,

for fear
of being hurt
they fall.

A PLACE

The wetness of that street, the light,
the way the clouds were heavy is
not description. But in the memory I fear

the distortion. I do not feel
what it was I was feeling. I am impatient to begin again, open

whatever door it was, find the weather
is out there, grey, the rain then and
now falling from the sky to the wet ground.

SOME ECHOES

Some echoes,
little pieces,
falling, a dust,

sunlight, by
the window, in
the eyes. Your

hair as
you brush
it, the light

behind
the eyes,
what is left of it.

FANCY

Do you know what
the truth is,
what's rightly
or wrongly said,

what is wiseness,
or rightness, what
wrong, or well-
done if it is,

or is not, done.
I thought.
I thought and
thought and thought.

In a place
I was sitting,
and there
it was, a little

faint thing
hardly felt, a
kind of small
nothing.

THE WORLD

I wanted so ably
to reassure you, I wanted
the man you took to be me,

to comfort you, and got
up, and went to the window,
pushed back, as you asked me to,

the curtain, to see
the outline of the trees
in the night outside.

The light, love,
the light we felt then,
greyly, was it, that

came in, on us, not
merely my hands or yours,
or a wetness so comfortable,

but in the dark then
as you slept, the grey
figure came so close

and leaned over,
between us, as you
slept, restless, and

my own face had to
see it, and be seen by it,
the man it was, your

grey lost tired bewildered
brother, unused, untaken—
hated by love, and dead,

but not dead, for an
instant, saw me, myself
the intruder, as he was not.

I tried to say, it is
all right, she is
happy, you are no longer

needed. I said,
he is dead, and he
went as you shifted

and woke, at first afraid,
then knew by my own knowing
what had happened—

and the light then
of the sun coming
for another morning
in the world.

GOING

There is nothing
to turn from,
or to, no

way other
than forward, such
place as I mark

time. Let me
leave here a
mark, a

way through
her mind.

THE CITY

Not from that
could you get it,
nor can things
comprise a form

just to be made.
Again, let
each be this or
that, they, together,

are many whereas,
one by one,
each is a wooden
or metal or even

water, or vegetable,
flower, a crazy orange
sun, a windy
dirt, and here is

a place to sit
shaded by tall buildings
and a bed that
grows leaves on

all its branches
which are
boards I know
soon enough.

WORDS

You are always
with me,
there is never
a separate

place. But if
in the twisted
place I
cannot speak,

not indulgence
or fear only,
but a tongue
rotten with what

it tastes—   There is
a memory
of water, of
food, when hungry.

Some day
will not be
this one, then
to say

words like a
clear, fine
ash sifts,
like dust,

from nowhere.

A REASON

Each gesture
is a common one, a
black dog, crying, a
man, crying.

All alike, people
or things grow
fixed with what
happens to them.

I throw a stone.
It hits the wall,
it hits a dog,
it hits a child—

my sentimental
names for years
and years ago, from
something I've not become.

If I look
in the mirror,
the wall, I
see myself.

If I try
to do better
and better, I
do the same thing.

Let me hit you.
Will it hurt.
Your face is hurt
all the same.

THE SHAME

What will
the shame be,
what
cost to pay.

We are walking
in a wood,
wood of stones,
boulders for trees.

The sky
is a black
sudden cloud,
a sun.

Speak
to me, say
what things
were forgotten.

THE STATUE

I propose to you
a body bleached, a body
which would be dead
were it not alive.

We will stand it up
in the garden, which
we have taken such pains
to water. All the flowers

will grow at its feet,
and evenings it will
soften there as the darkness
comes down from such space.

Perhaps small sounds
will come from it, perhaps
the wind only, but its
mouth, could one see it,

will flutter. There will be
a day it walks just before
we come to look at it, but by then
it will have returned to its place.

THE WINDOW

There will be no simple
way to avoid what
confronts me. Again and
again I know it, but

take heart, hopefully,
in the world unavoidably
present. Here, I think,
is a day, not *a*
but *the*. My hands are

shaking, there is
an insistent tremble
from the night's
drinking. But what

was I after, you
were surely open to me.
Out the far window
there was such intensity

of yellow light. But love,
love I so wanted I
got, didn't I, and then
fell senseless, with relief.

TO BOBBIE

What can occur
invests the weather, also,
but the trees, again,
are in bloom.

The day will not
be less than that. I
am writing to you,
wishing to be rid of

these confusions. You
have so largely
let me continue, not
as indulgence but

then to say I
have said, and will,
anything is so
hard, at this moment.

In my mind, as
ever, you occur. Your
face is such
delight, I can

see the lines there
as the finest
mark of ourselves.
Your skin at moments

is translucent. I
want to make love
to you, now. The world
is the trees, you,

I cannot change it,
the weather
occurs, the mind
is not its only witness.

THEY

I wondered what had
happened to the chords.
There was a music,

they were following
a pattern. It was
an intention perhaps.

No field
but they walk
in it. No place

without them, any
discretion is useless.
They want a time, they

have a time, each
one in his place, an
endless arrival.

A METHOD

Patterns
of sounds, endless
discretions, whole
pauses of nouns,

clusters. This
and that, that
one, this
and that. Looking,

seeing, some
thing, being
some. A piece

of cake upon,
a face, a fact, that
description like
as if then.

A SIGHT

Quicker
than that, can't
get off "the
dead center of"

myself. *He/I*
were walking. Then
the place *is/was*
not ever enough. But

the house, if
admitted, were
a curiously wrought
complexity of flesh.

The eyes
windows, the head
roof form with
stubbornly placed

bricks of chimney.
I can remember, I
can. Then when
she first touched me,

when we were
lying in that bed,
was the feeling of
falling into no

matter we both lay
quiet, where
was it. I
felt her flesh

enclose mine. *Cock,*
they say, *prick, dick,*
I put it in her,
I lay there.

Come back, breasts,
come. Back. The sudden
thing of being
no one. I

never felt guilty,
I was confused but
could not feel
wrong, about it.

I wanted to kill her.
I tried it, tentatively,
just a little
hurt. Hurt me.

So immense she was.
All the day
lying flat, lying it seemed
upon a salty sea, the houses

bobbing
around her, under
her, I hung on
for dear life to her.

But when
now I walk, when
the day comes
to trees and a road,

where
is she. Oh, on my
hands and knees, crawl-
ing forward.

PIECES

I didn't
want
to hurt you.
Don't

stop
to think. It
hurts,
to live

like this,
meat
sliced
walking.

THE CIRCLE

Houses in
the ring
to pass through,
past the

accumulated
sense of them,
I know
everyone.

I am
stumbling, my
feet are
awkwardly placed.

The man
who says
hello to me
is another

man, another
comes then. One
by one
the women who

look
after. In-
side the
thinking.

THE HOLE

There is
a silence
to fill. A
foot, a fit,

fall,
filled. If
you are
not careful all

the water spills.
One day
at the lake I took
off my bathing
suit

in the water,
peed
with pleasure, all
out, all

the water. Wipe
yourself, into
the tight
ass paper is pushed. Fatty

Arbuckle, the one
hero of the school,
took a coke bottle,
pushed it up his girl.

But I
wouldn't dare,
later,
felt there,

opened
myself.
Broken glass,
broken silence,

filled with screaming,
on the bed
she didn't want
it, but said, after,

the only time
it felt right. Was
I to force
her. Mother,

sister, once
seen, had breasts.
My father
I can't remember

but a man
in some building,
we were all swimming,
took out his

to piss, it
was large. He was
the teacher.
Everywhere

there is pleasure,
deep,
with hands
and feet.

I want
to, now I
can't wait any
longer. Talk

to me, fill
emptiness with
you, empty
hole.

A PRAYER

Bless
something small
but infinite
and quiet.

There are senses
make an object
in their simple
feeling for one.

THE FLOWER

Remember the way you
hunched up the first
times in bed, all your
body as you walked

seemed centered
in your breasts. It
was watching the world
come toward me, I felt

so alive and honored.
Me—least of all possibilities,
yet in bed before you,
the patient flower.

SAME

Why am I
the laggard, as if
broken charms
were debris only.

Some thought
of it, broken
watch spring—
is not rusted merely.

That is all
they talk of
in Madrid, as much
to say the same.

The same thing
said the same
place is
the same.

Left in pieces,
objectively—
putting it
back together.

THERE

A place so
hostile it does

not want
any more, not

even not wanting,
is there.

Would one walk
or run, or avoid,

whatever—at
that moment

a voice
so tense

trying to
be acknowledged.

JOY

I could look at
an empty hole for hours
thinking it will
get something in it,

will collect
things. There is
an infinite emptiness
placed there.

A PICTURE

A little
house with
small
windows,

a gentle
fall of the
ground to
a small

stream. The trees
are both close
and green, a tall
sense of enclosure.

There is a sky
of blue
and a faint sun
through clouds.

A PIECE

One and
one, two,
three.

THE BOX

for John Chamberlain

Three sides,
four
windows. Four

doors, three
hands.

WATER MUSIC

The words are a beautiful music.
The words bounce like in water.

Water music,
loud in the clearing

off the boats,
birds, leaves.

They look for a place
to sit and eat—

no meaning,
no point.

THEY (2)

They were trying to catch up.
But from the distance

between them, one thought
it would be a long time

even with persistent
running. They were walking

slower and slower
for hours and hours.

WAS

The face
was
beautiful.

She was
a pleasure.
She

tried
to please.

THE FARM

Tips of celery,
clouds of

grass—one
day I'll go away.

INDIANS

Big, wise
man. The happy
woman

in a place
she found. He
waited

in the clearing.

ENOUGH

1

It is possible, in words, to speak
of what has happened—a sense

of there and here, now
and then. It is some other

way of being, prized enough,
that it makes a common

ground. Once
you were

alone and I
met you. It was late

at night.
I never

left after that,
not to my own mind,

but stayed
and stayed. Years

went by. What
were they. Days—

some happy
but some bitter

and sad. If I walked
across the room, then,

and saw you un-
expected, saw the particular

whiteness of
your body, a little

older, more
tired—in words

I possessed it, in
my mind I thought, and

you never knew
it, there I danced

for you, stumbling, in
the corner of my eye.

2
Don't we dance
a little bit,

slowly,
slowly. My

legs
will work

to the tunes of
a happy time.

3
A distance
separates, ob-

jectively, as from
shore, water, an

island projected,
up, against

the sun, a smoke
haze, drifting,

reflects
the golden city

now. Your
head and hands,

your eyes once
in words were

lakes but
this is an ocean

of vagueness. The sun
goes out. I

try to feel
where you are.

4
Hoo, hoo—
laughter.

Hoo, hoo—
laughter.

Obscene
distance. The

mind makes
its own

forms, looks
into its terror

so
selfishly

alone. Such
a fact so simply

managed there is
no need for any

one else. All
by myself I see

the obscene bodies
twisting, twisting,

my hand
explores their

delight, un-
noticed, my body

shrinks
back.

5

One
by one
the form

comes. One
thing follows
another. One

and one,
and one. Make
a picture

for the world
to be. It
will be.

6

You
there, me

here, or is it
me

there, you
here—there

or there
or here—and here.

In two
places, in two

pieces
I think.

7

Your body is a garbage can.
Your body is white, why

let others touch it, why
not. Why

my body so
tentative, do I

like the pain
of such impossible understanding.

Your body
is a white

softness, it has
its own

place time
after time.

8

I vow to my life to respect it.
I will not wreck it.

I vow to yours to be
enough, enough, enough.

HERE

What
has happened
makes

the world.
Live
on the edge,

looking.

INTERVALS

Who
am I—
identity
singing.

Place
a lake
on ground, water
finds a form.

Smoke
on the air
goes higher
to fade.

Sun bright,
trees dark green,
a little movement
in the leaves.

Birds singing
measure distance,
intervals between
echo silence.

WATER (2)

Water drips,
a fissure of leaking
moisture spills
itself unnoticed.

What
was I looking at,
not to see
that wetness spread.

THE EYE

The eye I look out of
or hands I use,
feet walking,
they stay particular.

I wanted
one place to be
where I was
always.

I wanted you
somehow equal,
my love, one says—
I speak with that body.

But then it happens—
another time, a particular
circumstance—surrounded by such
a distance.

You took my heart
which was with you,
you took my hands
which I used for you.

Oh when regrets stop
and the silence comes
back to be
a place still for us,

our bodies will tell
their own story, past
all error,
come back to us.

OF YEARS

Of a few years
come into focus—
peace and understanding,
the uneasy virtues.

Of a mist.
A night's peace
waking to sullenness,
uneasy companion—

of force,
of coercion, compulsion,
of nagging, insistent
suspicion.

Of nothing
more than a moment.
Sudden candle light
shattered the night.

SONG

How simply
    for another
pace the virtues,
    peace and goodwill.

Sing pleasure,
    the window's opening,
unseen back of it
    the door closes.

How peace, how happiness,
    locked as insistence,
force weather, see sun,
    and won't look back.

FOR JOEL

Some simple
virtue of silence
you taught me once,
not to talk too much.

In your place, waiting,
up all night, talking
and drinking, flowers
for your wife then—

but not accepted.
The test was
how much unhappiness
either one of us could endure.

I think of friends,
some known for years.
There are men
made sense for me.

Measures—
ways of being in one's life,
happy or unhappy,
never dead to it.

Joy to the marriage, now,
of such a friend
gave me such reassurance
in his own pain,

joy to strength and weakness,
to what won't go dead
to its own pleasure
but likes to laugh.

A full shout
for happiness, a
bride of such delight,
a groom so wise.

A BIRTHDAY

Shall we address it
as you, lovely one,
singing those intervals

of a complex
loneliness, a wanting too
to know

its condition. Together
is one by one,
and a beauty

comes of it, a substance
of beauty—beauty, *beauty*—
dripping its condition.

I had thought
a moment of stasis
possible, some

thing fixed—
days, worlds—
but what I know

is water, as you
are water, as you
taught me water

is wet. Now slowly
spaces occur, a ground is
disclosed as dirt. The

mountains come of it,
the sky precedes, and where
there had been only

land now sticks and stones
are evident. So we are
here, so we are.

DANCING

To be dancer
of my own dismay,
to let my legs and arms
move in their own feeling,

I make a form of assumptions
as real as clothes on a line,
a car moving
that sees another coming,

dancing as all would
were it not for what it thought
it was always doing,
or could leave

itself to itself
whatever it is, dancing,
or better, a jerking leap
toward impulse.

A TALLY

A tally of forces, consequent
memories, of times and places—
habits of preparation at other
points of time and place.

And the hand found the fingers
still on it, moved the thumb,
easily, to the forefinger,
still worked. What

has come. Age? But,
to know itself, needs
occasion, as, no longer young
wants a measure.

The mirror the mind is,
reflective, in that guise,
long habit of much delaying thought
to savor terms of the impression—

it's not as bad as one thought,
but that is relative. Not as simple
as the boat is leaking, he, she, it,
they—or we, you and I, are sinking.

Within the world, this one, many quirks
accomplished, effected, in the thought,
I don't know how, I only live here,
with the body I walk in.

Hence I love you, I did, do,
a moment ago it was daylight,
now dark I wonder what the memory means,
loving you more than I had thought to.

No agreement to stay, see it out,
the dereliction of fleshy duties—
but not burn down the house
for whatever rage was once.

"OH MY LOVE . . ."

Oh my love,
in other times
the things we are
were beauty too.

In ways that were
I never knew
were possible
might talk to you.

Or on and on
and up and down
seasons and days
might make a place

unlike such
awkwardness makes
this one awkward
fall apart.

FRAGMENTS

Decorous, and forbearing further correction,
to the empty halls he announces
pardon. No wound deeper than
death, he says, not knowing.

———————

The fall of
feet dancing
to sounds within
his hearing. Oh,
how much he heard.

———————

Little song, sing
days of happiness. Make
a pardonable wonder
of one's blunders.